Dr. Madeleine Vieira's Anxiety Disorder Series
I'M AFRAID

Panic Disorder with Agoraphobia

Pablo Parrot
IS AFRAID OF FEELING TRAPPED!

Illustrated by Oxana Fomina

The right of Dr. Madeleine Vieira to be identified as the author of this work has been asserted in accordance with Section 78 of the Copyright, Designs and Patents Act
The book cover is Copyright to Dr. Madeleine Vieira.

Grosvenor House Publishing Ltd - Link House, 140 The Broadway, Tolworth, Surrey, KT6 7HT
www.grosvenorhousepublishing.co.uk

The book is a book of fiction. Any resemblance to people or events, past or present, is purely coincidental.
A CIP record for this book is available from the British Library.

ISBN 978-1-80381-701-9

This book is dedicated to my husband Christophe
and daughters Allegra, Alexia-Amalia and Eleonora,
with all my love,
and to children worldwide suffering from
from Panic Disorder with Agoraphobia.

Dr. Madeleine Vieira's *I'M AFRAID* book focusing on Panic Disorder
with Agoraphobia has been written
with the intent to help children suffering from these disorders.
She would like to note that although therapeutic children's books are a valuable
and much-needed resource, they are not a replacement for in-person therapeutic
treatment with a mental health professional.
While Dr. Vieira strives to help children overcome symptoms of anxiety
through her series, she shall not be held liable for any content in this or any
of her therapeutic children's books.

Introduction to Parents and Caregivers

Dear Parents and Caregivers,

It's easy to understand how difficult it is for parents and caregivers of a child with anxiety to cope with the situation. Their child's fear comes with an array of symptoms, such as a rapid heartbeat, dizziness, headaches, stomachaches, shaking, and trouble breathing. The child will go to great lengths to avoid triggers that bring these feelings on.

As parents and caregivers are a child's champion, you want to protect your child from these unpleasant and sometimes overwhelming symptoms.

You try to reassure your child. You try to help your child. You use logic and even allow your child to avoid the distressing situations.

Nothing works.

You may become frustrated and even angry at times as your child's anxiety controls his life and yours. You can't understand why seemingly ordinary situations frighten him.

If not addressed, your child's anxiety can worsen. He may not be able to go to school or have normal social relationships.

There is good news though! It is possible for children to overcome their anxiety. Through diligence and positive thinking children with anxiety can lead healthy and happy lives.

Based on the therapeutic technique of Graded Exposure, a component of Cognitive Behavioral Therapy (CBT), *Pablo Parrot Is Afraid of Feeling Trapped!* demonstrates that it is possible for children to manage their anxiety. The story guides children through steps that research shows help them overcome the harmful habits and patterns they've developed while struggling with their fears. Along with the story, there is an About Anxiety page that includes a list of coping strategies which can help alleviate anxiety symptoms.

If anxiety interferes with your child's life, please consult a mental health professional. Working in collaboration with a professional and letting your child know that you're confident he will be successful will give your child a stronger foundation and allow him to become his own champion fear fighter.

Warmest Wishes,
Dr. Madeleine Vieira

Pablo looked at the door. His heart raced and he felt hot and sweaty. He couldn't think straight.

"Are you okay?" asked Ollie.

"I-I have to leave." He shoved his way through his friends and raced out of the auditorium.

Pablo's racing heart slowed down.

"What happened?" asked Ollie.

"I knew I shouldn't have come," said Pablo. "This happens when I'm in crowds or when I feel trapped. I can't go to places like this anymore."

"That's awful," said Ollie. "I help children who have fears, like being afraid to be in crowded places. What if I help you overcome your fear?"

"I'd like that," said Pablo. "My fear stops me from going places and having fun." He flung his wings out. "If I wasn't afraid, I could go to the Mega Rock Concert the end of the month."

Pablo scrunched his face.
"What do I have to do?"

""Well," said Ollie, "one way to overcome
a big fear, like going to the concert, is to
face smaller fears first.
Then slowly work up to the big fear in
baby steps. Each fear you face is a little
more difficult than the one before.
Think of climbing a ladder, each step
helps you slowly reach your goal."

With his head tilted, Pablo asked, "How many steps are there?"

"The number of steps vary," said Ollie. "You can try as many as you like. How about trying six and see how it goes? Can you think of a first step?"

"Hmm," said Pablo as he looked around. "I can't think of anything that doesn't seem too scary."

"What if you walk through the food market?" suggested Ollie.

"I-I'll try. Is it okay if my friends come with me?"

"Of course," said Ollie. "I'll come too."

The next day, Pablo went to the market. "There are a lot of people. What if I get scared and can't get away quick enough?"

Charlie Cub put his paw on Pablo's back. "We're here."

VEGETABLES

FRUIT

LANTS

RADISHES

CARROTS

CABBAGES

APPLE

LEMONS

BANANAS

ORANGES

PEARS

FRESH
FRUIT
+
VEG

At the market, Pablo's heart raced and his legs felt shaky. "I have to leave," he said, dashing off.

His friends followed.

"Are you okay?" asked Ollie.

Pablo's face drooped. "I couldn't do it."

"It's okay," said Ollie. "You can try again."

"We'll go with you," said Sophia Swan.

The little bird didn't want to go back, but he knew taking small steps would help him overcome
his fear. "O-Okay."

Pablo and his friends walked through the market to the other side.

"I feel shaky, but I did it," said Pablo.

"Good job," said Ollie. "You deserve a reward." He handed Pablo a little pouch. "Each time you try a step you should reward yourself."

"Oh, sunflower seeds," said Pablo. "I love them. Thank you."

"After that," said Ollie, "you can practice Step 1 again. It's important to practice each step a few times before moving on to the next step."

"What might Step 2 be?" asked Ollie.

Pablo tapped his wing. "What if I go to a restaurant?"

Ollie smiled. "Great idea!"

"We'll all go," said Olivia Owl.

The next day at the restaurant, Pablo's stomach ached and his wings trembled. Gathering his courage, he went in.

Pablo whispered to Ollie, "I-I don't feel well."

"I understand," said Ollie, "but the door is right there. If you have to leave, you can."

Pablo ordered a bowl of soup. As soon as he was done, he raced out.

"T-That was scary," said Pablo.

"But you did it," said Ollie. "Aside from being scared, did anything bad happen?"

Fluffing his feathers, Pablo said, "Not really. And, I do feel good that I did it."

"Good for you," said Ollie. "Time for a reward. Then you can practice Step 2 again."

"The steps are hard, but I want to go to the rock concert.
Will going for a bus ride be a good Step 3?"

"Absolutely," said Ollie. "And, talking back to your fears helps build confidence.
You can also take slow, deep breaths to calm yourself."

YUMMY iN YOUR TUMMY

At the bus stop the next day, Pablo felt lightheaded. "I can't do this, Ollie. I'm a failure."

"Pish posh!" said Ollie. "Just trying is amazing and you deserve a reward for that. Want to try again?"

"O-Okay." Pablo took slow, deep breaths and kept telling himself, *GO AWAY FEAR*, as he got on board.

His heart raced when the doors closed and when they opened, he flew out.

"My heart pounded, but I feel good that I did it, Ollie. I'll practice Step 3 later."

"What about Step 4?" asked Ollie.

"It'll be scary, but I'll try to go to the movies."

Ollie spread his wings. "Yes, it'll be tough, but you've worked your way here with baby steps, and you've been practicing. You can do it."

Pablo's friends and Ollie went with him to the movies.

"It's not too bad in here," said Pablo. "I think I can handle this."

Just then a crowd came through the doors and headed to the ticket booth.

Oh, no, thought Pablo. His heart raced, his mouth felt dry,
and his stomach got queasy. *What am I going to do?*

"Are you okay?" asked Ollie.

Pablo's shoulders slumped. "I'm feeling more confident, but the steps are getting harder. I don't think I can do this."

Fluttering her wings, Sophia asked, "Is there anything else Pablo can do to help fight his fear?"

"There is," said Ollie. "Pablo, you can fight fear not just in what you *do*, but with how you *think*."

"Huh," said the little bird.

Ollie adjusted his monocle. "Let me explain. If you feel afraid and your thoughts are telling you it's scary, tell yourself you're strong. Tell yourself you're a champion fear fighter and you can accomplish anything you set your mind to."

"Wow!" said Pablo as he straightened up. "A champion fear fighter. I like that."

Walking into the movie, Pablo's heart raced.
He felt panicky. *I'm stronger than my fear*, he kept telling himself.
When everyone was seated, Pablo wanted to fly away,
but he took slow, deep breaths and fought his fear.

Clutching the arms of his seat, he sat through the movie.

When they got outside, Ollie tipped his hat to Pablo. "Well done!"

"That was really hard," said Pablo. "I'll play a game with my brother as a reward and practice going to a movie again. But I don't know what Step 5 should be."

Rubbing his chin, Ollie said, "What if you go to the mall tomorrow?"

Pablo's eyes grew wide. "Oh, no. It's huge. I'd be afraid I couldn't get out if I needed to. But I do want to attend the music concert. I-I'll try."

Outside the mall, Pablo stopped. "My heart is pounding and my legs are shaking, but I'm going to do this."

SHOES

WATCHES

CANDY
SHOP

AREL

Accesso

Pablo glared at the entrance to the mall. *FEAR, YOU DON'T SCARE ME.*
I'm a champion fear fighter. With slow, deep breaths, he was able to go into the mall.

SHOP 'TILL YOU DROP
SHOPPING MALL

"How do you feel?" asked Ollie.

"It was so scary, I thought I'd pass out. But I kept telling my fear to stop."

Ollie gave Pablo a wink. "I knew you could do it."

"Thanks, Ollie. I'm going to get a new book as a reward. And, I'll be sure to practice Step 5."

Lowering his head, Pablo sighed. "The concert is on Friday. It'll be too hard. Maybe I just won't go."

"You've got to go," said Darcy Deer.

"Yeah," said his other friends.

"Step 6 will be hard," said Ollie. "But what's the worst that can happen?"

"I-I'm not sure. I'll feel sick. I'll shake so much I'll fall down. I won't be able to get out."

Ollie nodded. "Those things could happen. But are any of them really horrible?
Concert arenas have a lot of exits. Why not just try?"

Pablo shook his head. "I feel braver, but I still have to work hard to fight my fear."

"That's to be expected, Pablo. Each time you accomplish a step, your fear weakens and you get stronger. In time, your fear will be as tiny as an ant."

"Okay, Ollie. I'll try."

Pablo searched the arena for all the exits. His heart pounded, he couldn't think, and his legs felt like jelly. "FEAR, STOP IT. I'm stronger than you. I'm a champion fear fighter."

Sitting with his friends, Pablo used all his courage
to get through the concert.

When it was over and everyone was exiting,
Pablo kept telling himself that everything was okay.

Once outside, Ollie high-fived Pablo. "I'm proud of you."

A feeling of victory welled up inside the parrot. "I DID IT! Thanks so much, Ollie, for being there when I needed your help. I really am a champion fear fighter!"

About Anxiety

According to Dr. Vieira, the number of children with psychological disorders is at an all-time high and of those children with a diagnosable anxiety disorder, the majority are not receiving treatment.

Anxiety is a feeling of worry, fear, or uneasiness. It can cause a variety of physical symptoms including, rapid heartbeat, sweating, dizziness, trembling, weakness, and agitation. It can often affect the quality of the sufferer's life.

While this may sound concerning, there are strategies that can be used to help manage a child's anxiety symptoms.

Cognitive Behavioral Therapy (CBT) helps children recognize their thought patterns and identify where and when those patterns help and where they hurt. In other words, how we think and act affects how we feel. Using Graded Exposure as part of CBT, a stepladder approach, the child slowly and systematically faces his fears and reduces the symptoms of his anxiety.

Panic Disorder with Agoraphobia

Panic Disorder is an anxiety disorder that causes children to have sudden and unexpected episodes of intense fear that leads to extreme physical and emotional discomfort. These episodes are called panic attacks and can last from minutes to hours. The sufferers can feel like they're dying. If they have an attack, their first instinct is to get help.

Agoraphobia is an anxiety disorder related to feeling trapped and is usually accompanied with a panic disorder. In particular situations or places, the child fears he cannot escape or get help if he suffers a sudden panic attack or his anxiety intensifies. This creates a feeling of being trapped, causing panic along with a feeling of helplessness.

In this *I'M AFRAID* book, Pablo Parrot wants to attend a Mega Rock Concert, but he fears getting a panic attack in open or enclosed spaces or crowds, such as at an outdoor market or the movies. Pablo worries he won't be able to escape or get help if he gets too panicky. To overcome his fear, he uses a stepladder process to gradually expose himself to situations that will trigger a panic attack. With patience and courage, Pablo manages his anxiety and reaches his goal of attending the Mega Rock Concert.

For more information on Panic Disorder with Agoraphobia, visit:
www.DrMadeleineVieira.com/books/imafraid/panicdisorderwithagoraphobia

To check out the other books in the *I'M AFRAID* series, visit:
www.DrMadeleineVieira.com/books/imafraid

About the Author

Dr. Madeleine Vieira is a Clinical Child Psychologist with a special interest in Childhood Anxiety Disorders and Infant Mental Health. She has completed a range of studies to post-doctorate level and is continually expanding her academic and professional development and expertise. She has attended universities in both the United States and United Kingdom, among them are the University of California, Los Angeles and the University of Oxford.

Dr. Vieira has lived in seven countries and currently resides in London, UK with her husband and three children. They have a Shih-Tzu called Caesar who barks too much when the doorbell rings and is nothing like the Emperor! Dr. Vieira's hobbies include, portrait photography, world travels, dancing, and languages.

Working in private practice, Dr. Vieira offers Cognitive Behavioral Therapy (CBT), Cognitive Behavioral Play Therapy, Play and Creative Arts Therapy, and Diagnostic Assessments to children. Along with this, Dr. Vieira offers Clinical Supervision to Play and Creative Arts Therapy trainees and professionals.

In addition to being a registered Clinical Psychologist with the Health and Care Professions Council (HCPC), Dr. Vieira is a qualified Test/Assessment User registered with the British Psychological Society (BPS). She is also an accredited Play and Creative Arts Therapist and Certified Senior Clinical Supervisor in Play and Creative Arts Therapy registered with Play Therapy United Kingdom (PTUK).

To add to her many credentials, Dr. Vieira is Cool Kids accredited by the NSW Education Standards Authority (NESA) which involves treating childhood anxiety through a specifically designed Cognitive Behavioral Therapy (CBT) program of which graded exposure is an essential component.

Specializing in the diagnosis and treatment of Childhood Anxiety Disorders, Dr. Vieira is passionate about alleviating symptoms of children suffering from anxiety. Her *I'M AFRAID* anxiety disorder therapeutic children's series was created out of this passion. Through this series, Dr. Vieira hopes to reach children worldwide, well beyond her practice, as well as have it serve as a therapeutic tool to other mental health professionals.

You can learn more about Dr. Vieira and her practice on her website:
www.DrMadeleineVieira.com

Coping Strategies

1. Tell your parents, teacher, or other person you trust about your fear.

2. Think positive: "I can face this fear and handle uncomfortable feelings."

3. Talk back to your fear: "Fear, I'm in control."

4. Fight fear not just in what you *do*, but with how you *think*. Imagine yourself as a champion fear fighter.

5. Take slow, deep breaths to make you feel calmer.

6. Remind yourself that the anxiety is only temporary; it will not hurt you, and it will pass.

7. Use a stepladder approach to manage your anxiety by taking steps to gradually expose yourself to your biggest fear.

   a. Decide on how many steps you will try to achieve your goal and overcome that biggest fear.

   b. Figure out what each step will be. List and number the steps on a piece of paper before attempting the first step.

   c. Start with small, less difficult steps (bottom of stepladder) and work toward bigger, more challenging ones (top of stepladder) until you reach your main goal.

   d. Before beginning, choose a reward for each step with the last, most challenging step deserving the best reward. Even an attempt that fails deserves a reward for trying.

   e. Practice each step several times, and only when you feel comfortable enough with the step, do you move on to the next one.

   f. Continue to use the other coping strategies as you go through each step.

8. It's recommended you seek help from a mental health professional.

Stepladder

Goal .... Reward ....

8. .... Reward ....

7. .... Reward ....

6. .... Reward ....

5. .... Reward ....

4. .... Reward ....

3. .... Reward ....

2. .... Reward ....

1. .... Reward ....

www.ingramcontent.com/pod-product-compliance
Lightning Source LLC
Chambersburg PA
CBHW042003100426

42813CB00020B/2964